D1602253

AMERICAN ODALISQUE

AMERICAN ODALISQUE

POEMS BY JANE MILLER

COPPER CANYON PRESS : PORT TOWNSEND

Grateful acknowledgment is made to The National Endowment for the Arts
for a generous grant which allowed me to complete this book, and to The
Helene Wurlitzer Foundation of Taos, New Mexico, for the space in which
to do so.

And to the editors of the following magazines in which these poems first
appeared:

THE AMERICAN POETRY REVIEW

THE AGNI REVIEW

THE ANTIOCH REVIEW

THE HIGH PLAINS LITERARY REVIEW

THE IOWA REVIEW

IRONWOOD

OPEN PLACES

THE PARIS REVIEW

PARTISAN REVIEW

PAVEMENT

THE POETRY PROJECT NEWSLETTER

THE SONORA REVIEW

TENDRIL

A broadside of "Intestine of Taos" was printed by Mummy Mountain Press
for Arizona State University, 1986.

The publication of this book was supported by a grant from the National
Endowment for the Arts.
Copper Canyon Press is in residence with Centrum at Fort Worden State
Park.

COPPER CANYON PRESS
PO Box 271, Port Townsend, Washington 98368

Contents

FOR BARBARA CULLY

Portable Shrine

You said you felt someone
in the room with us. Could we,
without perishing, without hurting
anyone, be innocent again?
As if, walking alone,
all places are the same.

AMERICAN ODALISQUE

Sycamore Mall

Coppola's *Cotton Club* starts at Campus Two Cinema Saturday 6:45 mall time.
The Negroes in the film are played by blacks,
playing opposite the tennis shop, tobacconist, lingerie & antennae sales,
a glass-cased elevator & automatic bank teller.
Because this is a strangeness tendered in others,
a display of the humiliated
& recast human being, a thing Michelangelo transcended by marble
in David with its oversized right hand,

because this is a tenderness strange in others,
I dine formally in a towel with day lilies & hydrangeas on the table,
fresh raspberries & roses in their second bloom,
then sympathetically go out on the town.

Symptomatically it is as if I am approaching the Doge's Palace in Venice
& the piazza is covered with ice.
I exit my hotel on the Grand Canal, Paganelli's,
& slide arm in arm with my lover.

It was right to act back then, in summer, as if I were living
a love story that would be simple, with its curious
nocturnal glow, not unlike the mall hybrid light,
where like a single thought there persisted
an electronic chant on the portable tape player
as from the bowel of the Basilica the choir repeats a benediction.
No one ever touches himself in public, Our Lord,
because we've all rubbed off on one another so much we're invisible.

That is what has become of the tree for which Our Mall received its name,
with hope that it won't be the end of the world if we act out
of our best mood, surprisingly delightful original sex
without climax, a gift reserved for the end of the century

for those who still live by the spirit
of an act, on a street prepped like a movie set.
It was right to act back then, & to trust the movement
of the affair to the relationship

& insist on perfection. It'll be a while
before we are hoisted & joined as characters on a screen in sepia tone
for a theater inside a mall under the influence of temperature control.
Painfully one day we wake & haven't the right
clothes for Venice. It has snowed as it did, we are told, once a lifetime
ago; the full evening moon floods the piazza & in the morning
workers haul benches for the tourists to pass over.
A simple pear from a painting, or the marble hair of the David,
bandages art places over our eyes,

survive in Renaissance books next to the jog & diet shelf.
Michelangelo & Giotto appear naked to the touch,
holier because no one is fully conscious nor ever able
to forget anything under the false light of the dome,
Our Ladies of the Air-Conditioner, the Air Freshener,
the Night Moisturizer. Between summer & winter of a given
year, I reflected on life to no end,
& fell in love, ourselves in a lover,
like art whose strangeness tenders a body in others.

Picnic

A mother and child activate the lawn,
the child in her sundress and the woman in white, barefoot.
Their Post Toasties are post-modern.
I sit closer to one of the speakers
that rests on the statistical curve of the backyard,
the long curlicue signature with the dot after it.
Every now and then I imagine
we could as easily have gone for a swim in the rain.
As long as we give someone a window
into our personal lives,
like how I spend the winter
in the desert and the summer by the coast,
somebody has to, then it's somehow
ok to be casual about the narrative.

Therefore casually in the grass
the violets paint the mother and child
with all of nature between them,
a dot of yellow shielding the sun.
This couldn't take place
on metromedia television, because the message
is the corsage the woman has on.
All form avoids recreation.
Memory has to have a good time too, at any expense,
the jerk who asks Who's the pimp here anyway?
and is a syntactic greeting.
Let's leave them alone, innocent, the baby
doesn't have to be a line nor the woman
a sentence. The yard explodes.

Near You Are Heavenly Bodies

I adapt the rhythms of my actions to the affairs of the earth
    maybe you don't want to be loved everyday and maybe I don't

is it arbitrary or is it intuitive?
    I'm just going out for a moment

a complete change of life and a profound rest
    shall I remember my beach as one reminisces about fame?

my father's tender direct kiss on the lips
    meaningless in the way someone thinks

I'm just going out for a moment
    but only suddenly

with no shirt the beautiful
    day coming onto night

fear or freedom when that's understood we build
    it isn't a matter of acquiring it's a matter of divesting

who were my friends   among whom did I move?
    yellow apples   green and red grapes   red and orange pears

all I want to preserve is the landscape
    a guy walks into a bar throws down $2 adjusts his nuts & orders

the end of the century cries out
      now tell me did you get up like this at night as a child?

on the pretext night wasn't made for children
      we have to prove we're honest

how did you know I belong there?
      a state as obvious as California

who was I stopping to ask is this real?
      the smallest creatures near you are heavenly bodies

natch! I'm just going out for a moment

Lengthening Day

The flowers are that someone else might enjoy them.

They lived together on and off for years, or they visited.
This was how some few people did it. And to
see them on the beach, it was as surprising and natural
as finding a watering hole in the desert. One got undressed
and swam.

Now the tide comes in, remember?

You know someone casually, for a short time, then before
you know it, while traveling, you see someone who reminds
you of her. Already memory bothers desire.

While thinking of you, I am observed by the passers-by.

What's that I hear about a missile base?

Then they rolled their jeans up, and soaked them to the
thigh anyway, the one who took off her red crewneck
had a white one underneath. First the line drawn was physical,
now it's mental. Between the lovers a blue anchored
catamaran, painted white inside. At ebb tide, walking gulls.

I simply see them on the beach, no trip about it.

I say something perverse and she takes it as a compliment.
I said, "Jaunty-phony but anyway likeable."

We're not different, we just have this double life, the day
in which things occur and the imagination in which they develop.

She complains, but it's not about fame or travel or love,
so I don't mind.

Early hours, long walk – we have it in memory. What has made
them so happy? There's the beach, that's taken for granted,
and the small sailboat, and the few articles of clothing.
Clear warm spring day. We can't live with it being described
to us.

That continuity in my life is an illusion. One surfaces
and shouts, "Cold!"

Topos

At the documentary level, a voice on tape
survives an instant, chatting about
politics, money and love, then is extinct.
The language is local and commercial.
It fractures a moment. On the screen,
meanwhile, on a darkened nightclub stage,
a star moves. One is not oneself
on stage, one enters an autistic drift
with music. For example, I hear storks
in the background, a whistle, an electronic
synthesizer, a metallic bird. It isn't spring,
but the organist plants seeds. Then I'm part
of the audience.

If I call and the phone monitor is on
they will hear me ask for her
and be able to talk about me while I'm talking.
Behind them is a South American
wood flute serenade. Sounds like wind
through empty Pepsi bottles. Heads swaying,
hands snapping. It's a devotional exercise
and the carnations and tulips in their living
room, couched like talk show guests, show them
watching TV, tourists at home. I call,
finally feeling at home in the motel,
listening to music, wanting nothing of my own,

everything to belong to my mate and my mate to me.

Outer Space

I didn't write for the simple reason
I thought of you constantly,
and I was bothered by it, and changed
my composition for two leaves
into a composition for two Jews.
And that's not everything,
because memory dies with a smile on its face,
leaving its head in the sea –
my body's powerful experience
without a name. It's not easy
making a circle completely in one's head.
The red dulce in the water is human brain.

Now the prairie is as quiet as you
in someone else's arms.
The god in the wilderness wasn't us,
the god in that sea breeze used us.
And the room is still hot with mid-day heat,
but the sun will set in an hour.
Becoming someone else's made me what?
An American who makes beauty
and anonymity interchangeable.
When we pulled out our single mat
to sleep on it, we got to know one another
forever, it was self-possession so disarming.

One dog, one very large dog, two dogs.
The one who orders Death aloft,
and the one who presses Death's bellybutton,
bombing installations and civilians,

the lover and beloved, pigs and fishes.
Earth is blue and yellow before
it's green. In my Sonnet to Keep a Secret
I wrote, "Spring is black at night,
where we went not wrong exactly, exactly
not right." In my Sonnet to Confess,
where I exit the loop of pleasure
in phosphorescence, there are no days

alike, like lovers.

Memory at These Speeds

I love these hours alone I do
        not
                like them. Like them, I am
slow to divine
                meaning from change, meaning
I love you & remembering
                        waking next
to you like a white gull against a white sky
                become blue
I feel detached, although I realize
this is the drift of happiness it is not
                my choice
                        yes I like you
for it. Faith

        for this moment is living
with a fear
                I will lose you or myself,
    each arousing
                the other,
eternity!
                that spectacular hour in the afternoon
        when you arrive & suck me
                        as if it were through time
we are reconciled
                or in dream,
        the desert we return to
        heaven
                all that disappears
        when we look back,
                        for this time we are lovers we are

moved by the sea
                in a studio with aqua floorboards
        & white lamps now like stars inhabiting a pattern
             now random.
Never let ourselves be subject
                   to either dependence again
or pain. Where once there were so many
  words we had to choose
              between us,
your sentence effortless as mine is fair.

I am on a peninsula
forty miles out in the Atlantic
and have driven my car to a mechanic
to replace its ball joints.
I left it in Wellfleet
and am walking every half mile
and crying and walking every other
the four miles out to the harbor.
When I get there I intend to
pace the pier and receive
the appreciation of the fishermen.
I have a mind to fuck
one for the afternoon.
This probably won't happen, and not
because I'm not good looking, and tender
in grief. Anyway the cry
has become more
like a detonation, dry, brief.
It's all right. I'm not doing this
to forget, and I feel great
humor and communion. Standing on this pier
where my own two feet had been
on similar docks in Amsterdam,
Biarritz, Nice, Athens, I remember my mind
wandered even then
from the two lovers I happened to
have, traveling the sun to serve
our ends. Tomorrow,
why the hell on earth
even bring it up, like a tide
brackish, effervescent, pink,

familial, I'll be back in town
with my freedom to come and go
geared to the misconception
I want to. I wrote a good
friend and fruit grower, Mary Fisher,
a few weeks ago, it's funny,
Mary, I'm on a red bedspread
in The White Horse Inn in America,
you're on the other soiled coast, California,
I'm talking *broke* and more beautiful
than that day you saw me leaving
my husband many lovers back,
feeling rummy. Christ: girls,
art, money, I'm thirty-three,
this isn't TV, and there's a war on.
Do you want to live
forever? Or is that poetry,
a wild iris I was sent,
wasted at The White Horse
powerless to a fault,
one for everyone.

Venus de Milo

I last felt this unthoughtful at age twelve.
It's cold for June, no wind, low tide, no moon.
I'm flat on the deck in a sweater on a towel.
Oysters on the half-shell, eh? A glass of wine, eh?
Foghorns, stars, about as much outer space as a weekend.
It's the promised land after the faded dream.
Now that we have learned to fly,
using portable butane-fired blasts,
when I wear black and my hair is full,
I can see my soul on the patio,
tired necklaces of lit coals
in a barbeque by the bay.
And I won't until I think of something great to do.

Like children grow, things change in spurts.
(The old charm bracelet sells for $115.)
Pandas appear on the new club ties at Polo/Ralph Lauren.
Who lives on what for a year?
The U.N. will devote x billion to the continent of Africa.
(Small Wonder Auto Focus Color Video Camera, $699.95.)
The West, of which we are a signature, will pay
over a third. (High-density floppy diskettes, price?)
At the simplest level of function,
our culture is about the best fitting jeans.
Concord grapes and MacIntosh label underwear.
If a single person can love
another, in as much as the world

as a day trip is nearly over (it's half past 10),
theoretically anyone can
shower and bike to the beach in the morning.
I still feel for the tourist

committed to under-consciousness.
In my blue frame, an airplane and a gull glide,
no different in size. In an earlier life,
I could prefabricate love
like houses in my mind, slump block and concrete.
Dismantle and reconstruct, void to a new location.
Tonight (microsoft), marigold flaps like a skin of moon.
Tenderness, yes, even passion. But to trust someone again
(in stretch fibers) will test how we are alone.

American Odalisque

Schwinn rests in back seat
of my blue convertible;
leaving, I'm sorry.

.

Snails sprawl fine sand, dawn
spills like waste into the sea.
I don't care either.

.

Mobil Station next
rest stop, where I phone my love.
Busy; no answer.

.

Coked & dancing, I
think of Cape Cod now, your voice.
Shivering barstool.

.

I'm safe now in town.
I sleep late with my new love.
Remember? Say yes.

.

Cool, professional,
like a river is a slave
for sun, I seek love.

.

Pepsi & money
flow easy; I need you here
while I am just past young.

.

I stall on the bridge,
press my emergency light.
Berkeley, a lifetime.

　　　　.

Midnight. Heaven is
bathing, the window open.
Just a kiss away.

　　　　.

Aren't they always
mistaken for images,
your Invisibles?

　　　　.

A coyote, bats,
they put me in no mood here,
I can't touch myself.

　　　　.

And think of the moon
who is my family since
I have no children.

　　　　.

Are fish unconscious
and mute? Last night I ate one
in lime sauce. Years pass.

　　　　.

My car, your shadows.
Roadrunner skids to the door.
My friends are scattered.

　　　　.

What will the new art
be made of? Dusk, a snowfall,
same cold human feet.

.

Easter Sunday sun.
Stewardesses picketing
United parade.

Stravinsky

It is on earth only you are apprehended,
where the palms sway beside a mylar sea
and the sky burns refinery orange.
Lonely, lonely, as always the sign-bearer
wears white, pushing a silver shopping cart.
My car is your car,
these things are settled
as finches settle on siding,
as fast food and trailer parks
replace home-cooking and home.

I'm sitting in a sun which on the screen
is reminiscent of yellow, and with the logic of dream
my friends discuss life. They say NON MERCI
in reference to. . . . They say DARLING, describe this,
and I begin, farewell, that beautiful word . . .

Instead of having daughters their age,
I simply see them on the dimpled beach,
the sand dappled, the wind daffy, the sky adrift.
I said I'd give it a year, a year was my specialty.
And we spoke of love, as familiar as mowed snow,
not at night, in the morning because in the morning
angels perceive the thing exactly,
only things can express a fact exactly.

Loving makes me conversational,
feeling the pressure of the archetype in make-up.
One can die as easily of loss of self,

or fry in the hammock in the tall grass by the sea.
We dream our death like
a hundred clouds over the extra suburb,
the thatched roofs sprouting TV antennae.
And no one watching
inside our heads, the refineries.
Death is like having a good idea.
It was ten o'clock, my darling had not yet called.

The Cover of Mars

The Lucille Ball–Desi Arnaz hour concludes
with a Fix beer slipping my neighbor's grip.
Again he will sleep on the cot in the vestibule
under a pile-up of stars. Now he shouts
at his ignorant self in Greek, and his wife.
Now that I am returned from the taverna
like change from an empty, I lie in the amphitheatric
vibrations of the alphabet of
international report and arthritic snore
pelting the strip of beach invisibly like moon drag,
white on white on decanted white forever,
having wandered out of three ouzos with dinner, wondering
whether peace with the Turks lasts
because war with one another continues
mentally, calibrated astronomically,
whether people's hearts are too sore to care
to reclaim territory, or whether I have not listened
or lived in such a way that I can understand
a strange country's fate, let alone
my own, wracked with mosquito at this juncture
of adult love, from this as from any altar, better
than from the shot of morphine
the doctor administers the last time
I freaked, cramped, I can blame
myself in your presence and claim this room
never had to do with my life, someone's
rotten smiling teeth above an undershirt like sailboat
mirrored upside-down in sea, lit in the courtyard
by the cerebral cortex of ultrablue cable television,
Lucille in flames, addressing Ethel's willing
slow-take, the enormous wash-out of beach, weed,
sea, sea, and sea, so that I can remember
my center, backyards of beautiful barns and junked cars,

32

the America I lose you in when we return,
with precision, and with my usual splash
as from outer space, years later, alone, I land
up on a given afternoon crossing
the Mississippi into Galesburg, Illinois, through
Carl Sandburg Drive, past cemented Penney's,
singing down Main with the church
bells of an historic cyclone, as one remembers
an old life lifted from an old notebook, as obvious
as our souls drifting the coast off Mars
or worse, your face on the cover of Mars.
I give you back my heaven. You're all in my head.

The Mate to the Plum

Shall I speak and light clouds?
                    May I see? Seeing,
is it the silk of nothingness?
               Let dawn crumble
and be milk by noon.
            Most brightly of all burned, my love,
now you can open acres of camomile
        as if in a rain that one doesn't win
with humid air but with semblances,
                  shadows.

They have their little castles on them in full view,
                   curved
like mother has a time called evening.
             I have an idea this is the sea,
is the sea, I think, patience?
          I think, this is time,
rock draped in black cloth,
        and only last year
to have been in front of it. That I touch –
           is touch so heavily judged? –

your heart under a shingle of the world,
            I find that once before
you opened.
       What if I am growing
back grief,
      as when I leave off thought
of the vows you have kept to me?
           Or else,
it's exactly as you said, long beach, walking to dinner, said,
     to have a thought stops breath,

a month of one day
                    more beautiful than the next.
Let the droning of the bulls on the moon decide for me
                         where no conversation served
to survive and farm the desert.
                         And these mountains you spoke of,
how the soul is the last day
                    you play for me the guitar
with its six paths over the abyss.
                    Having lost you everything returns rumored into being

like the truth, nuggets of rain moused down to the river
     as if there were a reckoning.
The blossoms have made me last here. Body of winter flowering,
          I come back to you as
milk streaks by beneath the moon,
                    as the tenderness of your not having to
see me this way, with my glass over time.
                                   If I ask
who's holding the sky, when will you replace it? If light fall,
     let the great unrestrained asterisks

wake you. I waited until the night before, believe me,
                    as long as I possibly could,
and in time approached dignity
     a large music to grasp but with my eyes
since you are gone and these are not our stars.
          I keep like pressed leaves
my hands over my heart when the water starts
                    sleeping in and out of time behind that
closed door, the door already closed
                    when I get up to go.

And these gold pieces flying off me – autumn
    I spend returning what's not mine,
the yellow bird, columbine,
      raven, black yellow black yellow bees, wasps,
evergreens.
        Trumpet flowers like us trying out old silver flutes
long ago, eager and dumb.
           Be comforted you are clear, my foreigner,
like a row of white sails joined
    by two red sighs, love words

I took my mind from to be here.
          I waited until the night
before, as long as I possibly could,
        and then I found them, your eyes
for windows: *You took a good look at me. You saw me. I know you saw.*
    Kind hands must be holding
them up, where drift the violets drifted lovers miss.
      It isn't far back to the house,
and your not being there in a borrowed wood bending the road
    is what I have

to love to love.

Centripetal

This time if there is time if time
embodies a true story, I'll tell you the truth.

So well do I know you
that were I blindfolded and led about the summer beach

I could tell what part of it I was
standing on from the perfume where you'd been,

that olive skin moist like the shore,
as a child the fairest in Athens, up early to escape

to school with your satchel in the shadowless glare.
Go friend. The southwest wind blows across the Cape

with the constancy of a parent, and the heart-shaped
air sacs ripen to iodine and a blackish-brown.

Everywhere the stony smell of dry sand and hot salt grass
should remind you of home.

What I thought all winter were pebbles I see now
are snails impregnated on the rock. I can smell them

three thousand miles away in Santa Fe like the one
thing you can't smell on yourself, your breath.

Although I don't get used to it, I think
of you making love with another with tenderness.

Among ponderosa and joshua, among juniper,

I play the piano attentive to the whole piece, like sky.

The sunset is lavender and gold, equipoised between three peaks,
slate, fire, and pearl. Stepping outside in the ashes

I call in the dogs, and with them a race of gods transformed
to maize gathering the meager end of summer rain.

These obsidian Apache tears I found in Sedona to bury
with you in the East. They say rather than die

by another, men leapt from the mountain weeping these
stones. I know how deeply one can look

into your eyes, and down there perhaps you must be
lonely without me. Among the mosaic

of the Taos range, proud Wheeler Mountain and the Sangre de Cristo
chain, yucca blooms like desire equal to the sun

rousing it. If memory serves me,
I cup your sculpted face and loosen

your hair as you stoop for the bath. I live
the risk of the romantic. Nothing can save me,

who takes leave of you for love
remains.

High Holy Days

I am the Princess of Life Gone Out
I am the sunless parallel in the vertical

Two spirits forming out of the quiet by day
& the native by night
Most demure, Jane
most meditative of you

to broadcast the velvet of an inner thigh
of the nymph in the summer sky
& for the last secret effect
before it goes out over the airwaves

tell me something equally heavy
which leads the dancers to the hanging
of their red-hot tights to the line
setting the sun

Now is the time, whichever you like better, friend,
all inferior beautiful thing

Her skin is whiter than milk   her tan is darker than beer
in the shadow of special dispensation
like for a Jew the absolute
saints sighing & fairies crying
all over their invisible members

Random cradle starting up like a life in me
Don't be surprised if I laugh the shore says to the water
every time you win in the end
but live where
since we didn't know of any place to stay
to take in an even smaller part of everything

a case of a sacred object
not making its escape toward evening
a cow
implanted in the video arcade of a midwest mall

a small head nobody will believe I did it
Saturday night after the movie let out
seized like a biker
with hazel eyes like headlamps turned yellow

If it's such a deep secret no one will verify it

Goethe has to describe the beautiful
folds of Christ's garment
raised off the ground exposing one knee
before we get a sense of internal space

automatic freaks like auto freaks through a wheatfield

In my heart I have a memory of you
but not the brain to decipher it

god the wind as windless as the world behind a computer screen

Out of the air-conditioned inferno in the broad street
high school girls bleach holes in the darkness of Clinton Avenue
I stand like Ozymandias on Quaalude
missing whom I miss

once in reverence & once in despair I dreamt
we got both harbors

Iowan

Let me wake level in the moonlight, Lord,
even if you send a chopper & motorcycle
& it seems an inopportune moment for parting,
while I am bedded in Jockey shorts
refashioned in a special dispensation for women.
Better far would be the coming-on of rain
than dull sobbing desire overspread with phantom
light laid upon some sheety lake,
O troubled brown halo,
loyal to a lover on each coast, O precarious sag.
Blessed & aggressive is one night mower.
Like a cow implanted in a video arcade
alone am I grazed as the sacred
by night, out over the airwaves, unballast wing.

Miami Heart

In a long text, on live TV, in an amphitheater, in the soil,
after the post-moderns, after it is still proven
you can get a smile out of a pretty girl,
after the meta-ritual lectures,
after the flock to further awareness bends "south,"
and Heinz switches to plastic squeeze bottles,
as one flies into St. Louis listening to Lorca's "Luna, luna, luna . . . ,"
beyond Anacin time,
after, God help us, the dishwasher is emptied again,
and Miss America, Miss Mississippi, reveals she has entered a hundred pageants
since age six,
Packers' ball, first down after a fumble,
the corn detassled,
the assembly of enthusiasms awakened,
and we meet in a car by the river
not not kissing, considering
making love, visiting Jerusalem, the awful daily knowledge
we have to die in a hospital on the sixth floor, in a lecture, on live TV,
or in an amphitheater at half-time,
at one's parents' condo, over pasta,
in a strange relative's arms, in debt, along the coast, staring
at a lighthouse, the heart bumping, bumping the old pebble up the old spine,
a squirrel scared up a sycamore by an infant,
along this stench of humility, along that highway of come,
charge-card in hand,
I shall give my time freely
and the more I dissemble the more I resemble
and the more I order the more I reveal I hide,
the better, the faster
I sleep the more I remember
to go elsewhere,

a movie, excuse me, now I must whisper
not to disturb the patrons,
now I must drive, now park, tramp to the edge of the world,
roughness, ferocity, cannibalism,
bite, chew, transmogrify,
inside the lungs the little revolutionaries, between the thighs the reflex
it's too this, it's too that, it's not enough,
similarly, and more particularly, it's raw twice over,
it's the imagination draining its husks, left-handed,
because comparison is motive, which is why
one writes with one's desire.

Betrayal

As long as it's August, we can think of November as a snail's shell.
Because I'm falling in love with you, you know.
In Athens, in a stranger's apartment, hearing bouzouki music
like tin birds until the police come to break it up.
I never felt at home in the family.
Blue body, white car.

Can you imagine, I have been living
with so many lovers over the years and you don't know a thing about it,
I'm sorry all over the place.
I'm your whisper, I'm your free wheel. It kills me,
my father picking pennies off an old rug,
bunching newspapers into a ball, hurling a few feet away, hell,

I'm only able to write this sentence once.
Is it after all your power which prevents you
showing up posthumously scarved and hooded?
On feastdays, on horseback, on a cloud, yesterday.
Yours already, can't you drag your long gabardine
from the demimonde to the tip of my face?

I'm not after meaning, I'm after you.
Such a song, the black bread and the moon
in a brusque transition to reality.
Don't let me tire myself out on an impulse.
Remember me this way, dawn mute and clear. A cloud hung in a tree.
As if all of a sudden you don't have any possessions.

Don't you see, it's the horrid good fortune that comes from the grief
of others, someone watching us between touch and tenderness
like animals. But speeded up in dream, passing cars, your top down,
your tape blasting the very words spoken by a fountain and repeated
by the sea. We shall probably never . . . but why say it?
Fingering that ends in leaves of oil and gasoline, inexorable leaves.

44

Sunset Over Hand-Made Church

Like,
people get emotionally tied to
the first person who
fucks them up
the ass,
       god willing,

we were driving toward Biarritz
& stopped to call Alexis,
exhilaration in our voices
as we described the scenery, an emotion
akin to Carlos Williams's
man swinging a shirt over his head
or Hass's shouting hello
              to an empty house,

& as
the one pleasure of the traveler
holding a lemon to his nose on a windless day
               is to know he can leave,

the week we saw Arles
we enlarged everything
out of our minds,
Arles exactly as painted by Van Gogh,
the goldenrod, wheat, apple trees,
no one
tending them in all the hours we drove,
for the French, odd,
          not a soul,

the difference being
we had each other & were still
believing in a god,

ménage à trois, the next day slept between mountains
where the proprietor caught trout
& we ate in the poised and spirited
style of women alone
among men in the immaculate
dining room,
          like a picture of a country dining room serving rose pears.

What a night in a featherbed
in a room with a high ceiling,
life has been good, good, finding
our empty purse & providing
the wine we drink under a quilt.
          I did not want anyone to see that my face was so happy,

because I had slipped into the face of my dead,
who know so precisely what to relive
with their heads calmed
like a unicorn in the lap of a virgin,
                    & through me drive through France

with you, this mental self who
buys a paper & crosses the square for a beer
in Tourrette-sur-Loup, scaling the terraces of the olive
trees after lunch
          to play the wooden flute.

It's this distance from you,
this freedom we have to forgive,
that keeps us on a tether
          like goats, exactly like

ghosts.

Return of Serve

Drunk on the threes, morning, noon, and night,
                           it seems foolish
to sentimentalize what in its own right remains
flawed and anyhow passes
                         like a plane over an ocean,
                                 the European continent, the Mediterranean,
mammalian, distant,
as old as the vine itself
                         the steady intimation of failure
                         breaking its juices on a ridge, your mouths,
which I inhaled as if sex had a meaning, setting.

In time you appear close
and chaste, your chestnut and fair hairs tied,
                         and I would see my joy from both –
                                       had I eyes
to see the rest would be fantasy – those hours upstairs
                         nights dying couldn't touch,
                               nights lit by candles we call on
earth *heaven,* those chants I tell myself
                         while I go there again to be able to
                         say holy nights to fall
asleep – in this culture how to get away
                                  with saying,
on the breath of a devil and an angel – and not know
                         one from the other, who I was,
                             nor care to because impossible to
love one better.

I've come to love only what I have to do.
I've come to love the light
                         finding myself
among shore birds.
                         Even if I could with a thousand wings . . .

nothing returns.
                    If I thought dying,
                          if I could write my way
out. I hold you here because hope says to,
because she is so simple in her expression,
                              sitting on that pier now
                                    with her dress covering her knees
in the manner of custom
                          or mourning.
There is nothing erotic in hope, so we imagine
                          she too will make herself come
away from that promontory
to sell strangers her drug
so we don't have to trust her, so we finally admit nothing
                          is pure.
                                    I am
in my thirties now where I might be enjoying
                              labor, independence, travel,
until you are less
someone new I have to
love everything
                    to death.

You other, remembering
how you perfumed
                    your sex, lowering your eyes to your ashes,
                                              after that,
everything is incidental, a thousand pardons
nothing, and for each one if I could,
                    the ones I pick up and walk home without touching,
the miseries if I could convince myself
go away, dutifully, go away,
                          even this single tear in the wrong
season, wasting time, if.

I want to be right
                   and I don't know how to
say this modestly, hope
is cruel, in the end it's just
                        one truth among many that you must safeguard
a place where you wish to be
                        someone else's lover?
                                    Square one,
what is it after all but a light
                        touch one desires
to carry around
            like a sandpiper a shell,
a vain thing
            dropped into the bay at dusk,
which I hear as if
                – for god's sake and not to recognize –
the sun
        had a meaning, setting.

                    Godawful rot
on the beaches of whales
                    too big to break all the way up,
                            de-composing,
as in song, in a world they may have thought
        to sacrifice for. It's just like me to wake
                                    late, alone,
addressing the last to go
                    as if I were dressing a wound,
measuring, counting
                    on the most calloused cries to finally leave us
with a supreme distrust of suffering
                            jealousy,
the especially simple pain of the self and the other
            more symphonic arrangement of the mass.

49

Mona Lisa

If it clears, I'll get out of bed.
The bay brays, the sky is shark gray.
This is my voice talking,
but it's me watching,
both the TV and myself very consciously,
careful to keep the distinction.
My god, how things have changed.
One day we're dating and then,
shocking like a shark,
she's exactly with child, x,
and I think, because I'm crazy
enough to try it, why not?
Then I'm on a plane, I have to disabuse her boyfriend
of any notion he's the father,
and I'm sitting in the non-smoking bin
listening to my WalkMan, which will be a word
no one fifty years from now will know.
I take a personal blanket down from the sky.

Her boyfriend is a modern
peasant in jeans and tanktop.
And by the time I get back to reality,
I realize she'll always love him more than me.
A sharp ear pop.
And I had to traipse all over the island
to find him at his job in the bar,
she was a million miles away, in her twenties,
and all that about to be changed.
Sifted through the spheres of one eyeball.
And that is why I have not one chance in hell
except maybe to evaporate correctly when the time comes,

and why hell is dramatic, hell is time.
A thin coat of metallic paint covers the face,
and the rest of the body blue acrylic.
Horses, swordsmen, a trumpeter in a white robe,
an American soldier who stole a tank,
all in hell, all self-absorbed,
smiling the smile of a baby,
or one who trusts one's face to the sea.

Submission

Kazantzakis' walled grave
overlooks the city
you return to now
in the hour of love.
Your young man
rushes the dock with his olive branch.
The miracle is
not one of us is saved.
The lyrical and metaphysical
loneliness I feel
is as sweet as the fruit of a nut,
were there fruits or nuts on the trees.
This winter when we met
I supposed so.

From the mountain I climb to bed I see
who farms the moon for the hydrophants.
In the morning I fire the battery
under my hood, shuttling
from car to car in a spring storm,
drawing my hand back
from the mild shock.
What is art that cannot feel
even the rays of the sun,
those that are weak
and bring to life
those that are strong
and meant to submit.

Destiny

I am eating cold Chinese
in Joy's friend's flat.

I have been trafficked like a drug
planted by a child in Oaxaca,

like the story you are happy
without me, a lie I believe

you believe. And I am traveled
like the mercies on Telegraph,

the streetlamps burning down
the throat of this thoroughfare in Berkeley,

which gets us off
where I lived in the sixties and now

see my name in a window
and find its theme

useless in the act,
where had I not been

so privileged then
I would have had hope

well-humped for a quantity
of uncut drugs.

Out of the city
on Joy's cocaine

where it's always the freeway & the hour
the bars close & no English spoken,

where men chain to each other
as to an idea, say, that prayer

is as useful as a condom
against the current cancer,

here is the black Mercedes
of an acquaintance, top down,

and with the stars tight against my body
like a drunk I am singing

because in a war you taught me
your people flaunt a joyous will.

You who have raised fairness
to an exquisite pitch

which sounds like the wrong gear,
is it fair

to go on as the everpresent
red light we run

parts its mouth for a tongue,
three queens high on Stevie Wonder

crying *Where were you when I needed you
last winter?*

Now that it is morning
and the only person I know

drives by in his cab,
my name on his red lips the sun,

I call back
every minute the speed of the hours

of the days of summer, *Friend,*
not naming him, remembering his name,

and that's how it's been,
one with the universe,

blanking out at the Art Institute,
an expensive drug,

piano-brained, cleared to black and white
like a spaceship to another galaxy, M-TV,

while you are happy with someone
somewhere there

is the same crying and laughing,
two peasants,

the one you are and I become one
day when we aren't dead

to each other. I hear the story
of a stripper from her mother,

how she'd studied with the National Ballet
that when the lights go on you don't

pretend, you're alone.
I love you.

Romeo Void

I ask her it's supposed to be an easy answer will you stay?

In the pale overnight there's no difference
between our first and last days together
soon we'll tell each other so

we untap in what I call my bed
although I'd never slept in it
already light and sound

Mostly I am healthy and I run and what if I only find moonlight?

Insane for a year and never looked it up to see what it meant
Months listening as the sea determined to be motion and not weeping

I don't know if I save a moth
or kill it lifting it from the water

I go like a satellite
so close I can almost say what you mean to me
how else but in another's arms

Are you thinking of me by the river as I begin again?

nearest the light with my back to it

.

His idea of fun was belting his wife I'm telling this
to my friend and her husband about a total loser
I heard talk in a restaurant
I who never married and have no taste for it

This body that I'm in this time I love you

and only accept death from the inside like a woman

Like music just outside what I can imagine
this is being written by a different person this is better

written by a different person as in Poland my grandfather
a young man acts out a decision to leave his country

like someone biting a man's nipple
                                        and forces me over here
like a bed shoved from the wall with one leg

Marigolds eyebright rye saffron goldenrod
permission to write about anything and mention any place

extremes of ordinary where betrayal doesn't exist
                depending on the way that you feel

you live

each difficulty so close to dream

You are more beautiful than human to me sometimes god forgive me
everything seems pretty good all right

I'll have to return with a sprig of lilac but I'll be back
I have to return with white blossoms I'm gone I've left shore

as I left childhood
like a bed shoved from the wall with one leg

as one separates from the sea
for hot humid days and humid nights

asking whether I'm to have children
disregarding how
a person gets antsy
and then desperate for the internal life

So it isn't me so I'm not you all right

How quickly the little wooden flute fills with my heat
blowing across it the black ink that spells out the latest rage

an art out of a list of things loved

I have to return without wondering how others do it
I have to return without carrying rain
without the infinite loop that carries the family name

the half-light of sleep on the apples in Poland
the electrical short in the heart

as the rain lets up the slightest
birds start off in the air

tide fog white decks gulls as you can see from your window
I move by the line moral imperatives are physical

you at your desk in shirt and underpants
sleeping on a train eating someone else's food is it all right

I'm taking so long to leave you
happy in myself without gender forced to move on

memory I love you even if it's left from some dirge

the planets drifting like albumen

   y'all y'all fuck me now on the astral stubble
that bright red cardinal in the deep green pine
it's still getting dark it's still not night

I'm delighted not thinking about being one with the universe
this time I never even saw I bent and mended it

this body that I'm in this time I love you
as a beautiful woman even as a man might

think of me by the river I'll think of you by the sea

Timing for What

                we call the sound of someone
otherwise engaged,
                mid-morning of another perfect sky
when a cod is caught &
                decompresses too fast,
                popping its eyes out,
this season which was all appearances,
                whoever wasn't you,
                your affection
without desire, what I saw
                as betrayal
        is survival & a pleasure
forged
        out of our minds
                where love has been too
prepossessing like a mountain, emotionally
                exhausted,

                rock mined into pebble
destined to dent the river, the rivers themselves
                mortal
        figurations, ants eating
        so many times their weight,
white oars, blue fishing boat, scruffy waters peopled
        with summer, purple martins, meadowlarks,
                which I made up
                        my mind must be landscape
freely moving
        my heart, the only cell left
                to the birds as they tore the paper
sky from day to night
        always feeling the life
                of perished things,

                    by your leave
                                as it were.

                                I'm small if I climb
back to bed, skywriting long disappeared.
                    The bluffs are a mile from here,
                                and thankfully not our fault.
I sat next to a slug for an hour, an hour,
                                            how do I know?
                    Life resides outside the mind
                                without reference to afternoon,
& there are pods & pods of it, & music & art also,
                    like Picasso
            is a stone formed by a human hand,
                                the polite bird you may arrive
lightly like your perfume!
                    effacing
            my ego with tremblings I play on
                                            the piano for salvation
who'll bring you back,
                    angels too light to flex the hammers.

Let Three Days Pass

Let the one released from feeling,
merged in the neutrality of doing,
let him be the image of God.
Turn the channel to him, focus,
and let him float across your screen,
allied with mass culture.
I saw it, right on TV, and
I taped it on VCR. The color oozes
into reality even now, at midnight, during the
lightning flashes for which He is famous.

Nothing looks this good but really
the technical imagination makes it so.
Don't you think?
Here's a final minute, boundaries removed
and lightning on the sacrificial stage.
Eternity is caring for others,
the worst winter ever, where one does not exist
in a landscape but in an obscurity

exactly as lousy as the core meltdown
of the Brother nuclear facility. The first
two thousand die right away. And
the others, the Polish schoolchildren on the border,
the Rumanian schoolchildren and the schoolchildren
schoolchildren wait fifteen years,
showering every two hours and scrubbing their hair.

Video Rain

I am flown to your good side now.
Hiked up like a skirt,
the elevator intones
the cardiac, the cancer ward,
& finally the stroke floor,
like we're always in bed & need to be reminded
we must all carry our seed in our heads like flowers.
The insane staking an identity on high-tech.

It's time to rethink the entire landscape while I still have the body for it.
After years of doing what you've done, you'd do it too, my hero.
As I drag you to one side I wait for the coin to drop
& the video to begin lighting its commands,

ATTENTION this is your stress test,
having to really give all that suffering up,
having it as a guide, not a destination.
Everything is explained in-flight.
I can't stand these elderly stewardesses,

computer tones whispering FORWARD.
At Atlanta International there's a sharp tear of fluorescence
on a poster baby & in eyes that have just come from the freeway
as from a marriage of Mobil & McDonald's.
Getting off at the right time like a drug,

at Terminal C Olympic games are rerun,
blank sharks the pool, *blank* scarfs Wheaties.
This is consciousness of 5 p.m. airtime,
where temporarily I live

on the corner of Asamblea de Dios & Destino.
There's my exit, low tide, a last morning on a beach, & this is
it, isn't it, the earth we despaired of with Texaco
refineries & acid rain & you're having to take the hand

of the man in the moon, the black male nurse so clean
& necessary. Like tourists reach for a Holiday Inn in the fog,
as you feel for him I have been really feeling this
country lately deciding what to do next,
conscientiously pressing street crossings
like the accordion which opens into a city,
and the only difference is this really happened.
For everyone, Dad, the days are long,
but it seems like we're always in bed,

sunsets outside quiet silent towns.

Approaching Forty Devils

I love the attention. As I was saying the other day,
if I could explain just once –, I was unhappy

& staring at a weak sun. I would jog the shore in the morning,
my hair would be wet all day. It still gets in the way, curly.

I miss you terribly. I have your clothes on as the desert cools.
Earlier I was reading in the open room

& had to shield my eyes & unfasten the window.
And to think it's January. Ten or twenty years from now,

when I'm the same, without make-up, without shoes,
in an unmatched outfit & loose shirt, will I know you?

One day you wrote I made you feel, in no particular order,
grateful, generous, interested, capable & calm. I thought

of the responsibility of relationship, although I'm the one
who said, "I have proven my independence at too great pain."

Also said, "I never felt like a woman in this culture,"
and there's the matter I have to live with certain feelings never gotten over,

that I shouldn't have destroyed five years with my last lover.
It was then I knew I was tired of creation,

final breaks & strictly sexual acts, like the sun & shore indulging
a voice only more slavish talking to god.

I no longer wish to be obscure, as the rain that is rare here
is like rain, only more rare,

forced to remember the tide which I wept,
my tired feet, & a sun which was bonfire to my branches.

Peace Lyric

In a dream of sex & blindness,
boats grow rare on a river.

In a meteor shower which I feel but can't see
(like I sense there's something in the future

though I don't feel it),
the tossing of plums & grapefruit.

At the pole dance at Picuris,
a sheep tied to a pole.

At Santo Domingo, dancemasters & clowns attend a line
of elders & children;

a breeze floats down, an elder escapes with a story in his hands & feet;
in the morning I learn who was awake.

Arhythmic beats from turquoise & white deaf & dumb
drums, olive & gold painted,

dark-skinned, when they rest they rest on their sides.
– & I will be dead, this will have been me –

not to my homeland, although that too, nor a lover, exactly,
nor others surely, nor water & skyline, those too,

but to that absolute lure, intuition,
a coal sunset after diamonds

from the incremental gazes of the maiden dancers.
From the gazes of the dancers,

the laughter of my young lover
for those who want to know

all I will know of having a daughter.
At this altitude

grasses sprout like headdresses on the roofs of adobe, & in them
the dream of a blustery day in a city.

Under the wheel
on the High Road to Taos, deconstruction, de-mystification, demolition,

the unexpected downpour daily at four or five.
No longer harassed by my passions, hunter yellow & spring yellow,

violet blue, light gray,
there comes to pass like midsummer through a mountain

cheerfulness, sorrow, serenity.
No one go with me.

Ozone Avenue

These days I love to dream,
then I go hear *Romeo Void.*

It's a gentle hell, beloved.
Teen-age boys with lead guitars

singing a number like
there is no like,

you're gone.
I suck the little megawatts of my memories

which are nothing
exactly like mirrors

in a bar in a different mentality,
L.A., Albuquerque, Berkeley,

queens drunk and coked to the teeth
for the imprimatur of the closing

bells. I imagine
I do you

riding toward my fascination
the speedway, and the next minute

the next minute
sniff jasmine no one sees.

I lose the image of myself the rest of the world has
to catch up with. How long are you going to be

the rest of the world? One long day
the lover you left me

for returns to sleep
with you, you can't do it, it's ancient,

like talking
about sex and not realizing the lead

singer has one leg squeezing the other around a mikestand.
Knowledge is useless,

Heaven in script on a turquoise sweatshirt,
with Private Clubs for Los Ojos.

Where is this room?
Just a sweater with nothing under it,

a blanket with the design of the future.
I can see how she is because we only just met.

So used
to living intimately sometimes I wake

feelings in others I don't know.
Mornings the prostitutes

on Mission in halter tops and pumps
ignore me like I'm just another

voluntary miscarriage of an intellect.
Forever is getting faster,

air
traffic no one hears over a beach.

You make a small gesture on that beach, love,
flicking volcanic ash off a cigarette.

To Remember Every Hour

Eternal morning from La Siesta Hotel.
Three or four Mexicans blurt out a fight below.
I remember you shelling filberts with your teeth.
Now it is summer in December,
like a soul come from the shower
headless, a towel around its waist.
I don't really have to wear this lipstick
but to prove I'm alive I like the color.

A maid waits on me in some skewed reality
and I ask myself how I'm going to think.
This was my belief, to oppose something solid,
on the basis of night,
on the basis of fog.

Now in the distance my attention
is broken off like a bus horn,
like every hour I have to die
for fear I will lose you.
You know the feeling. It comes to you,
eventually to you, you,
mass that is no friend, month that punishes earth.

O why are you weeping, tell me why are you
unfortunately in the world?
Unfortunately in the world, pain
is the weapon everyone gets,
missing the northern migration.
No excuses please. Things we carried to their extreme

will meet again, the senses may be elevated
to sacred. Why live in principle
and die in fact? Clinging in English,
on the roof of Mazatlán
on the basis of night,
to prove you're alive.

Lost White Brother

We are about
to move away from guys getting messy
at their headquarters two tables down.

The you is gone, the bar vacuum is on,
the TV turned high,
casting a sunset on the opposite wall.
In the intelligent Taos Inn, a copy
of the historic Ansel Adams photo, *Moonrise,
Hernandez, New Mexico,* hangs.

Like, dehydration city,
like, work, like the spirit ants aren't going to move
out of the bowel of the valley, the ski resort.
If I go home I can sidle up to my bed
and arrange it so I slice the moon on my pillow
for the official margarita of the lost white brother,
hailed by prophecy. Lorca died this same age, 38.
Some people's parents are still alive,
and there will be that to deal with;

and I have approached this close like a date, like a feeling.

Don't think you're alone
in needing to be alone.
Whether it's his last egg Mandelstam offers Akhmatova
upon her return, or my beer, my refrigerator open to you,
& you've seen my picture, you know who you're dealing with,
we are the same lost white other, obligated
to hold the sun up in this culture until it rests

on the opposite wall like last night,
my love.

O'Keeffian

Through the window the piñon
with its precious nut

each which must be picked and peeled
by hand darkens in bloom,

and the old dogs called in
sleep, and the soft adobe cools

by lamp to crimson
and, too, darkens.

I am in love and no one I know
for a good thousand miles.

What the hell,
freedom to scale,

nor anyone to call to.
For months I have lived for the day

I could reconcile my anger
with my wish simply to start over

as your lover. And now with my heart
content as the ancient ocean,

both figured into desert
and alone, I release you as heat

transforms the apricot and peach
trees painted on the desert

of the year I hurt,
each beetle, centipede,

black widow, what I am
supposed to look out for,

like the rattler,
who contains my death

more than any other
I also love and more since

to love is to love the most
feared on this red earth,

with its heaven dark
blue like I imagine the mind

because the body doesn't have to
question day all night

nor the invisible
moon on whom I practice

your face.

Fiesta

A look has taught me these things –
as out onto a dark mesa
or, above, that pink sky,

Hispanics in egg-blue crinolines, cinched waists, 4″ heels
wail Christian rock, bursting with song like Pepsi spray,

bandilleros with children on their hips & shoulders,
the youngest scarved to a leg –

has taught me to stand with the others in public,
to clap with the drunk,
a look has taught me the lyric
in the black teeth of corncobs, gold teeth of sun.

I look & walk because I'm still not too old to be picked up,
male bikini lines visible in their jeans
I look at what they've got.

And not because there's no place to sit down on the hot rock of the plaza,
not because I'm a Jew gringa or with a girl,
a look has entered me from behind, like an idling Ford
bleeds oil on a terrified slab behind Arby's

at night, where wait the carbohydrate girls who have sworn on the cross
not to be home late in North America.

Intestine of Taos

The dirt part of the road is five miles.
Left up short steep hill, left. Second definite Y
road winds round, road follows pole with two black arrows.
Where there is only one.
The first time you're frightened,
then you can't live without it.
Several windmills confessing *I need you,* once or twice.
But it does not happen twice.
O ocean,
I'm sorry I met someone
when I was with someone else. Straw in the walls

and thunder every afternoon.
When it is noon,
the poor pooling of men in the state penitentiary.
Along the onyx leg of the drive to Albuquerque,
painted cars and nails along the freeway,
lone view, the dirt road and the tiny branch.
But this is not that branch, nor sun in the afternoon.

This is not heat. This is the brain walled,
the church at Ranchos de Taos
exorcized fifteen angles in the sun.
Wind on the corrugated metal eyes, on the hoarse
stalled motorcycles, the motels of love.
On a Saturday, on a Thursday, all afternoon.
Violent beauty, is that what beauty is about?

passed psycho pick-up trucks,
a windmill on the right,
this is that dirt part of the road,

whether love, in certain cases, mightn't be superfluous.
And immediately after that ardor, this technicolor plum
hastened to that dusk, those friends, one other.

It is unusually cool for July, not for a moment have I forgotten
the infinite tiny poem bolting the arroyo,
the fable of the red,
the drench of the white,
the felony of the yellow,
the cleavage of the black

cool summer night in the desert; boulevard of stars.

Broken Garland of Months

AFTER FOLGORE DA SAN GEMIGNANO

For November I give you the little Latin moons *lunaria,*
     hauling water from town without spilling
     the beautiful sounds of the words themselves, little

moons. May you compose a poetry of the tasks of this world
     in a privacy that is so amorous and does yourself
     so much courtesy, it is like the last great days

of a courtship whose flower always pollinates your wrist.
     In the mist, get a good idea and do it. Inside the
     pumpkin may you carve the flame.

For October I give you all holy the bell of the deaf, bells
     of alarm and delivery, one if the red squirrel hunts a
     mouse, two if the mouse finds a home. One if the chill

sits down at the table. My brow is flushed. I'm wearing
     my orange sash, hurry. Or maybe it's better with you
     gone, a bird who escaped the gaze its beauty invites.

Someone far away has made a decision in your favor.
     Or perhaps it's only kite-play, making infinity's
     sign that the old and the new pass in and out

of each other forever. For December, a hundred-fold late
     harvest, acres with apple and pear picking an hour's
     work, and round about you so you are never weary,

dancers for amusement before your every day of study.
Let sunsets regard you as god's maiden too dreamy
to go home or on. I give you a lover who wakes

waiting, who lies down beside you and is pasture.
And who stays up sometimes craning after a few
fireflies for fear you might cross and not come back.

Sympathétique

The magnetic moonlight
the metallic moonlight
I turn up the thermostat on Dodge
February zero & I down a Special Export
You're out confirming the dimmer switch an all-night light
an alkaline moon a chemical moon

The graveyard stones name several unrelated Millers
3 blocks from Dodge I bussed past them in a blizzard
this early evening with the children from the retarded school
down the street the street snowed in like a canal
A case like Van Gogh is impossible today
there's a filter on the sun
the snarled moon the journalistic moon
I am a sentimental lover
who would sit through a storm to paint the horizon
the charcoal moon the whey moon

Driving your car after your evening engagement do you feel glamorous
you are and I can't wait to touch your face and neck
who would lie down and love the earth and the earth tones
your dark auburn hair to the shoulder and your creamy belly below
rosy white
Above all else the figure the figure in the landscape
In church? even in church the figures in church
the potato moon the moon of the poor
Vincent punk Vincent victorious Vincent the Bohemian Vincent the great
But I want it to make sense it's about love
I want to announce that each time we go down on each other tenderly

we learn something we
hike out in late autumn or early spring before really
the earth's opened up hands stiff embracing three paint tubes blue red yellow
earth in the cemetery minerals like jewels
and I don't think How bad is the pain?

It's portable it was born in February green red black yellow blue brown gray
The temptation is to stand out in a June rain and enjoy it for itself

Biographical Note

JANE MILLER was born in New York City and has since traveled America extensively, living and working in New Jersey, Pennsylvania, Vermont, Massachusetts, Iowa, California, and currently Tucson, Arizona. During the early 80s, she traveled to Holland, France, and Greece, producing her most recent collection, a collaboration in the prose poem with Olga Broumas, *Black Holes, Black Stockings* (Wesleyan, 1985). She has two earlier works, *Many Junipers, Heartbeats* (Copper Beech Press, Brown University) and *The Greater Leisures* (Doubleday), which won the Open Competition of the National Poetry Series. Her awards include a National Endowment for the Arts grant, a Vermont Council Arts grant, and the Discovery Award. Her poems have been featured in *The American Poetry Review,* among other journals. Jane Miller has taught at Goddard College; Freehand, a learning community for the arts in Provincetown; The University of Iowa Writers' Workshop; and now is with the writing program at the University of Arizona.

The cover image is "The Great American Nude #4," by Tom Wesselman, courtesy of the artist and The Hirshhorn Museum and Sculpture Garden, Smithsonian Institution, Gift of Joseph H. Hirshhorn, 1966. (Photo by John Tennant)

The type is this book is Bembo. Typesetting by Fjord Press Typography.

Designed by Tree Swenson.

Manufactured by McNaughton & Gunn.